00
EASY
CHECKMATES

ABOUT THE AUTHOR

Grandmaster Larry Evans, one of America's most celebrated chess authorities, is a 5-time USA champion and author of more than twenty chess books including *New Ideas in Chess, Test Your Chess I.Q., Chess Endgame Quiz*, and a collaboration on Bobby Fischer's classic *My 60 Memorable Games*. He is a long-time contributor to *Chess Life*, and his syndicated chess column, "Evans on Chess," has appeared continuously since 1971. Evans has beaten or drawn games against six world champions: Euwe, Karpov, Petrosian, Spassky, Smyslov, and Fischer, as well as dozens of the world's top players.

Evans first won the Marshall Club Championship at age fifteen and the New York State Championship at age sixteen. He won the USA Closed Championship five times (the first time in 1951, the last time in 1980 – a remarkable span), the USA Open four times, the 1956 Canadian Open, and had numerous wins at many other opens including first place at an international tournament in Portugal in 1974. Evans represented the USA on eight Olympic teams (including the gold medal team in 1976) and served as captain in 1982. Evans was the youngest player to capture the nation's highest chess title at age nineteen, a record surpassed by Bobby Fischer at age fourteen. He is sometimes referred to as "the Dean of American Chess."

00 ASY HECKMATES

Larry Evans

CARDOZA PUBLISHING

Cardoza Publishing is the foremost gaming publisher in the world, with a library of over 200 up-to-date and easy-to-read books and strategies. These authoritative works are written by the top experts in their fields and with more than 9,500,000 books in print, represent the best-selling and most popular gaming books anywhere.

FIRST EDITION

Copyright © 2003 by Larry Evans
- All Rights Reserved -

Library of Congress Control Number: 2003109491
ISBN: 1-58042-121-0

Visit our web site—www.cardozapub.com—or write for a full list of books and computer strategies.

CARDOZA PUBLISHING
P.O. Box 1500, Cooper Station, New York, NY 10276
Phone (800) 577-WINS
email: cardozapub@aol.com
www.cardozapub.com

TABLE OF CONTENTS

INTRODUCTION

"Chess is a mind game, the objective of which is to checkmate or kill the opposing king. Ultimately that is the only way to win, unless an opponent, staring inevitable defeat in the face, voluntarily opts to resign. It is no surprise that throughout the ages chess has attracted both political and military leaders, including Queen Elizabeth I, her father, Henry VIII, the Russian czars, Ivan the Terrible, Peter the Great and Napoleon."
— British grandmaster Raymond Keene

The word checkmate derives from the Persian *shah* (meaning "king") and *mat* (meaning "dead"). Thus, the king is dead. But his majesty is never actually captured because one side wins if and when the opposing king is attacked but has no legal escape.

The purpose of this book is to teach beginners how to use 100 basic patterns for achieving checkmate. All the positions I show here are from real tournament games that took place after 2000. Be sure you take the time to work through the mating process for each example – it's the perfect way to improve your chess game immediately!

The Basics of Chess Notation

Before we begin looking at the checkmates, it's important that you have a basic familiarity with chess notation, a simple way of recording moves in a chess game. Chess notation starts with looking at the chess board as a coordinate grid. Take a look at the diagram below.

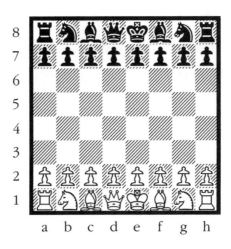

The horizontal rows, called ranks, are numbered from 1 to 8. White's first row is always number 1, which makes Black's back row number 8. The vertical rows, called files, are lettered from a to h. They go from left to right (looking from White's perspective).

With this grid system, we can refer to any square on the board by name. For example, White's queen is now on d1. Black has a bishop on f8. When you become a more advanced chess player, you will also learn how to record moves using chess notation. For the purposes of this book, though, I will write each move in plain English to ensure that you fully understand what's happening at all times.

BASIC MATING EXAMPLES

The Fool's Mate

A fool's mate does not refer to a chessplayer's spouse. It's simply the quickest way to win, and it requires just two moves. Take a look at the diagrams below.

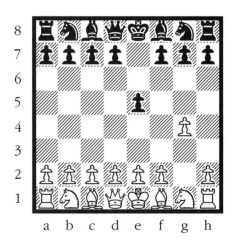

1.   White's pawn on g2 moves to g4.
       Black's pawn on e7 moves to e5.

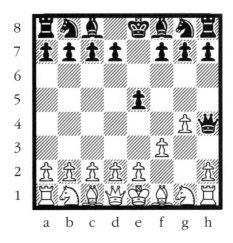

2.   White's pawn on f2 moves to f3.
      Black's queen moves to h4 for checkmate.

The Fool's Mate works only because White erred so badly in the opening.

BASIC MATING EXAMPLES

The Scholar's Mate

Another popular trap that might work for you a few times is called the Scholar's Mate. It requires four moves:

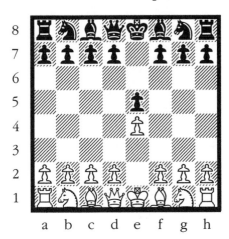

1.   White's pawn on e2 moves to e4.
       Black's pawn on e7 moves to e5.

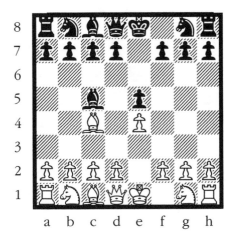

2.   White's bishop on f1 moves to c4.
       Black's bishop on f8 moves to c5.

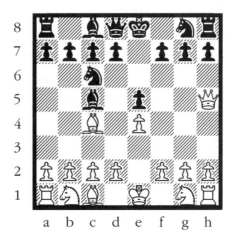

3. White's queen moves to h5.
    Black's knight on b8 moves to c6.

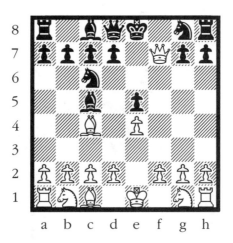

4. White's queen moves to f7 for checkmate.

Notice that Black can easily thwart the Scholar's Mate if, on the third move, he instead moves his queen to e7.

BASIC MATING EXAMPLES

Mates by Castling

Possibly the earliest example of mate by castling took place in New Orleans in 1854. Paul Morphy, a 17-year-old, used castling to defeat his father, Alonzo Morphy, in the following situation:

White mates in one move!

The solution is for White to castle (king moves to g1 and rook there crosses over it to f1), and the Black king has no way out.

Another example of mate by castling could have occurred in a famous game between Edward Lasker and G.A. Thomas at the London Chess Club in 1912.

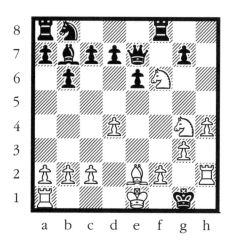

White mates in one move, in two possible ways.

Lasker chose to move his king to d2, yet castling queenside would also do the trick. Which method do you find more pleasing?

BASIC MATING EXAMPLES

A Veteran's Error

If you imagine that veterans are immune to overlooking simple mates even with plenty of time on their clocks in serious tournaments, then consider this sample.

Szabo-Reshevsky, Zurich 1953

White mates in two moves.

Szabo actually moved his bishop from b2 to capture the bishop on f6 (in error) and the game was later drawn. He missed a win by pin with:

1. White's queen captures the pawn on g6 for check. (the queen can't be taken because it's illegal to expose the king to capture from the bishop on d5; thus the pawn on f7 is said to be pinned).

Black's king goes to h8.

2. White's bishop on b2 takes Black's bishop on f6 for checkmate.

OR

1.   White's queen captures the pawn on g6 for check.

Black's bishop goes to g7.

2.   White's queen takes the bishop on g7 for checkmate.

"One does not look for a mate in two against a grandmaster," explained Szabo.

Summary
Although the goal is to checkmate the enemy king, don't expect an early knockout. You must conduct your attack methodically, and often fuel it with sacrifice of material to expose the enemy king.

The next chapters contain 100 more examples of situations in which checkmate is possible in just a few moves. The answers are available at the end of the book, but see if you can solve all of these yourself. Early diagrams are easier than the later ones, but you should have little trouble solving them all as you gain experience along the way.

Go to it!

MATES IN ONE MOVE

See if you can solve this first group of diagrams. In each one, White should be able to achieve checkmate in just one move.

Jakubiev-Ginsburg, Germany 2002

Diagram 1

Your Solution:

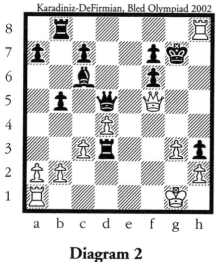

Karadiniz-DeFirmian, Bled Olympiad 2002

Diagram 2

Your Solution:

MATES IN ONE MOVE

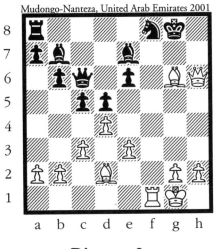

Mudongo-Nanteza, United Arab Emirates 2001

Diagram 3

Your Solution:

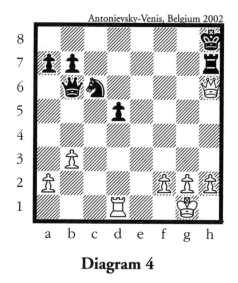

Antonievsky-Venis, Belgium 2002

Diagram 4

Your Solution:

MATES IN ONE MOVE

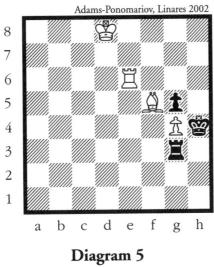

Adams-Ponomariov, Linares 2002

Diagram 5

Your Solution:

Banas-Cibulkia, Slovakia 2002

Diagram 6

Your Solution:

MATES IN ONE MOVE

Korchnoi-Solak, Switzerland 2001

Diagram 7

Your Solution:

Czebe-Koneru, Hungary 2002

Diagram 8

Your Solution:

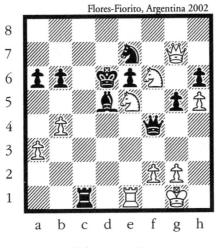

Flores-Fiorito, Argentina 2002

Diagram 9

Your Solution:

Iordachescu-Fernando, Italy 2002

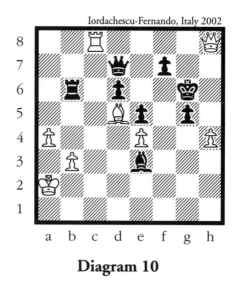

Diagram 10

Your Solution: (look for two ways)

MATES IN ONE MOVE

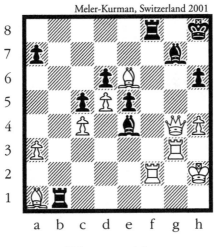

Meler-Kurman, Switzerland 2001

Diagram 11

Your Solution:

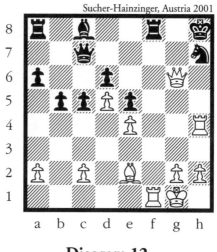

Sucher-Hainzinger, Austria 2001

Diagram 12

Your Solution:

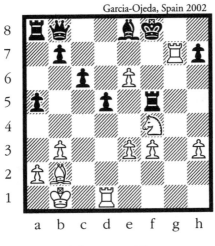

Garcia-Ojeda, Spain 2002

Diagram 13

Your Solution:

De Vreught-Van Wissen, Holland 2002

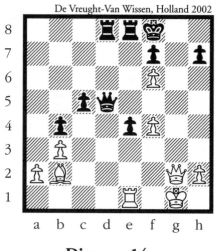

Diagram 14

Your Solution:

Kashgalev-Pushkov, Italy 2002

Diagram 15

Your Solution:

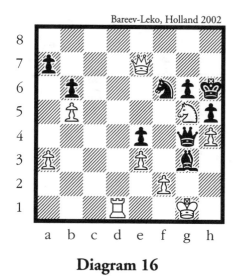

Bareev-Leko, Holland 2002

Diagram 16

Your Solution:

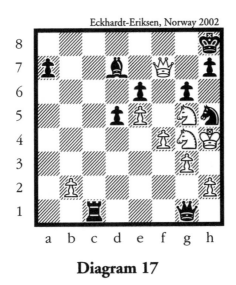

Eckhardt-Eriksen, Norway 2002

Diagram 17

Your Solution: (look for two ways)

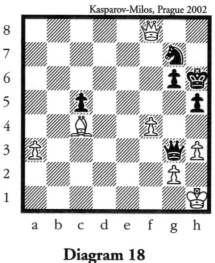

Kasparov-Milos, Prague 2002

Diagram 18

Your Solution:

MATES IN ONE MOVE

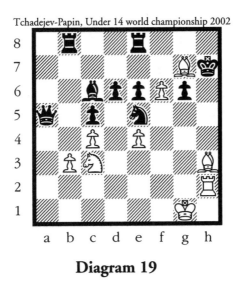

Tchadejev-Papin, Under 14 world championship 2002

Diagram 19

Your Solution:

Konguvel-Pour, India 2002

Diagram 20

Your Solution:

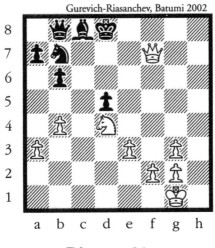

Gurevich-Riasanchev, Batumi 2002

Diagram 21

Your Solution:

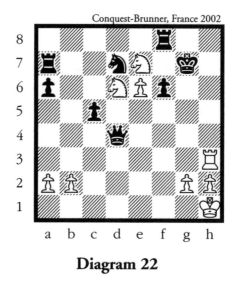

Conquest-Brunner, France 2002

Diagram 22

Your Solution:

MATES IN ONE MOVE

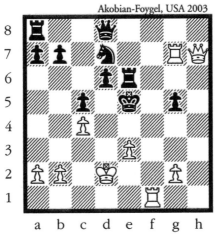

Akobian-Foygel, USA 2003

Diagram 23

Your Solution:

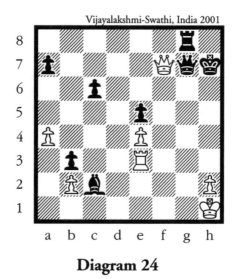

Vijayalakshmi-Swathi, India 2001

Diagram 24

Your Solution:

Vogt-Wirthensohn, Switzerland 2003

Diagram 25

Your Solution:

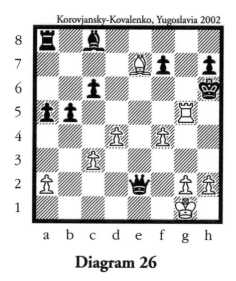

Korovjansky-Kovalenko, Yugoslavia 2002

Diagram 26

Your Solution:

MATES IN ONE MOVE

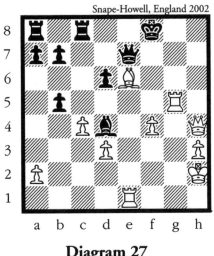

Snape-Howell, England 2002

Diagram 27

Your Solution:

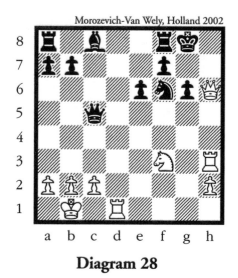

Morozevich-Van Wely, Holland 2002

Diagram 28

Your Solution:

Claussen-Mortenson, Denmark 2002

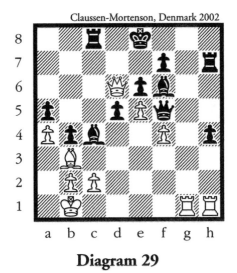

Diagram 29

Your Solution:

Let's make your task just a little bit harder. In each of the next group of diagrams, White should be able to achieve checkmate in just two moves.

Adams-Borowikov, Greece 2002

Diagram 30

Your Solution:

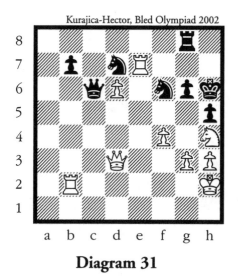

Kurajica-Hector, Bled Olympiad 2002

Diagram 31

Your Solution:

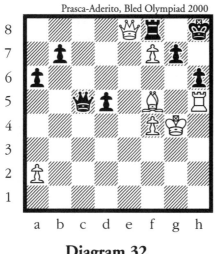

Prasca-Aderito, Bled Olympiad 2000

Diagram 32

Your Solution:

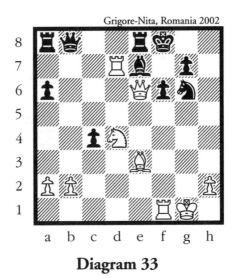

Grigore-Nita, Romania 2002

Diagram 33

Your Solution:

Lupulescu-Markov, Spain 2002

Diagram 34

Your Solution:

Gonzalez-Alvarez, Cuba 2003

Diagram 35

Your Solution:

MATES IN TWO MOVES

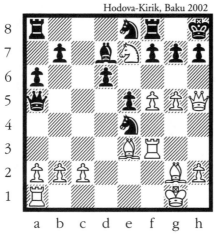

Hodova-Kirik, Baku 2002

Diagram 36

Your Solution:

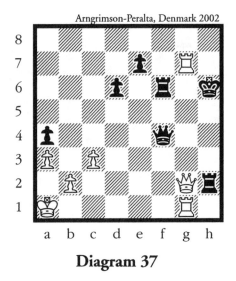

Arngrimson-Peralta, Denmark 2002

Diagram 37

Your Solution:

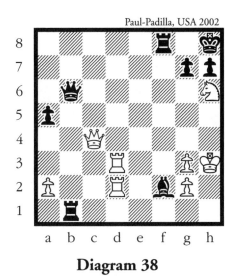

Paul-Padilla, USA 2002

Diagram 38

Your Solution:

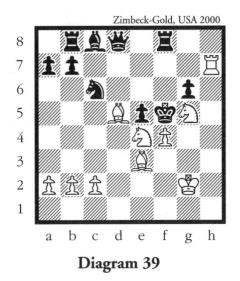

Zimbeck-Gold, USA 2000

Diagram 39

Your Solution:

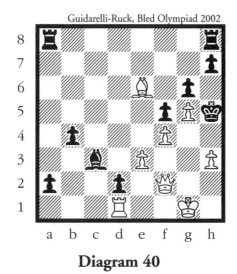

Guidarelli-Ruck, Bled Olympiad 2002

Diagram 40

Your Solution: (look for two ways)

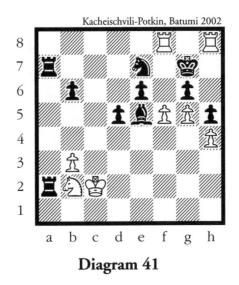

Kacheischvili-Potkin, Batumi 2002

Diagram 41

Your Solution:

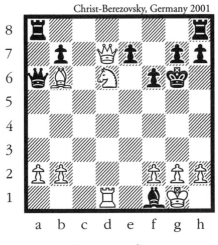

Christ-Berezovsky, Germany 2001

Diagram 42

Your Solution: (look for two ways)

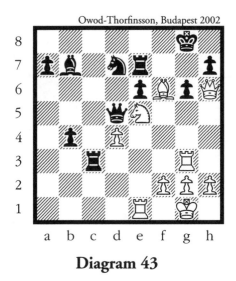

Owod-Thorfinsson, Budapest 2002

Diagram 43

Your Solution:

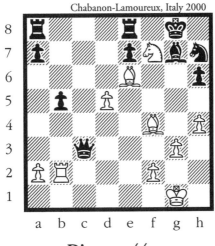

Chabanon-Lamoureux, Italy 2000

Diagram 44

Your Solution:

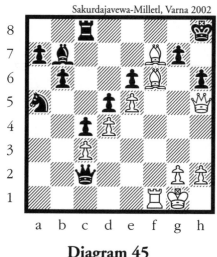

Sakurdajavewa-Milletl, Varna 2002

Diagram 45

Your Solution:

Matwejewa-Repkova, Varna 2002

Diagram 46

Your Solution:

Czarnota-Tomczak, Poland 2002

Diagram 47

Your Solution:

Biolet-Trapl, Czech Championship 2002

Diagram 48

Your Solution: (look for two ways)

Beaumont-Tiller, England 2002

Diagram 49

Your Solution:

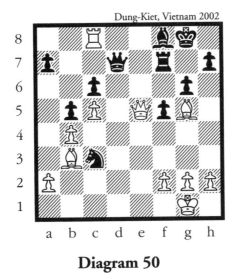

Dung-Kiet, Vietnam 2002

Diagram 50

Your Solution:

Paschall-Rouleau, USA 2002

Diagram 51

Your Solution:

Schenk-Lotscher, Norway 2002

Diagram 52

Your Solution:

Yamarellos-Kordis, Greece 2001

Diagram 53

Your Solution: (look for two ways)

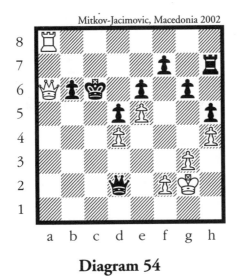

Mitkov-Jacimovic, Macedonia 2002

Diagram 54

Your Solution:

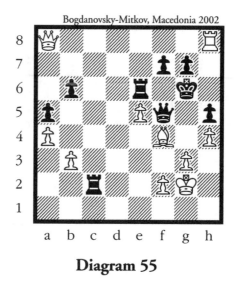

Bogdanovsky-Mitkov, Macedonia 2002

Diagram 55

Your Solution:

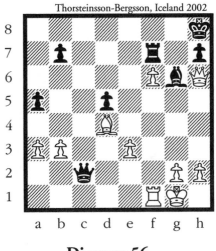

Thorsteinsson-Bergsson, Iceland 2002

Diagram 56

Your Solution:

MacIntyre-Fernandez, USA 2002

Diagram 57

Your Solution:

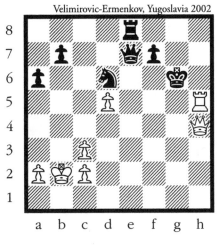

Velimirovic-Ermenkov, Yugoslavia 2002

Diagram 58

Your Solution:

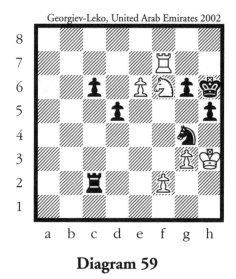

Georgiev-Leko, United Arab Emirates 2002

Diagram 59

Your Solution:

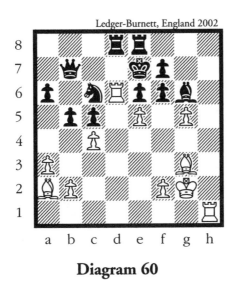

Ledger-Burnett, England 2002

Diagram 60

Your Solution: (look for two ways)

Shredder-Gulko, machine vs. man match 2002

Diagram 61

Your Solution:

MATES IN TWO MOVES

Petraki-Petsetidi, Serbia 2002

Diagram 62

Your Solution:

Dimovska-Jovic, Serbia 2002

Diagram 63

Your Solution:

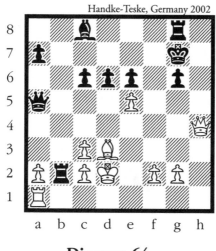

Handke-Teske, Germany 2002

Diagram 64

Your Solution: (look for two ways)

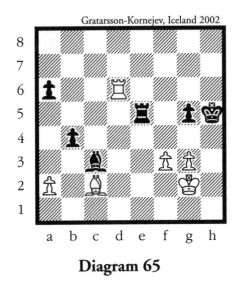

Gratarsson-Kornejev, Iceland 2002

Diagram 65

Your Solution:

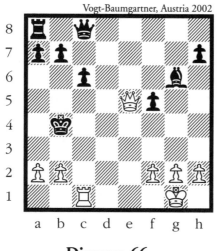

Vogt-Baumgartner, Austria 2002

Diagram 66

Your Solution:

Kasparov-Ponomariov, Linares 2002

Diagram 67

Your Solution:

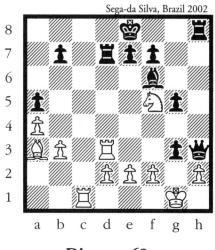

Sega-da Silva, Brazil 2002

Diagram 68

Your Solution:

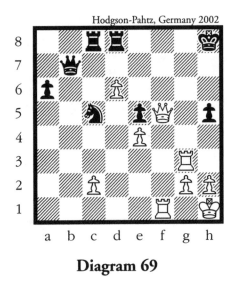

Hodgson-Pahtz, Germany 2002

Diagram 69

Your Solution:

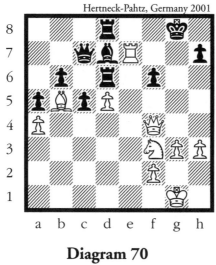

Hertneck-Pahtz, Germany 2001

Diagram 70

Your Solution:

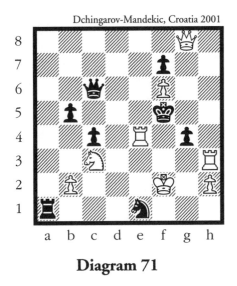

Dchingarov-Mandekic, Croatia 2001

Diagram 71

Your Solution: (look for two ways)

Golubev-Chenkin, Germany 2002

Diagram 72

Your Solution:

Itkis-Manolache, Romania 2002

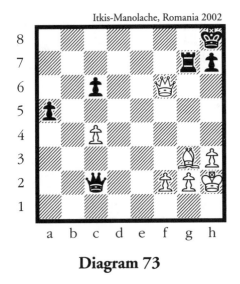

Diagram 73

Your Solution: (look for three ways)

Bacrot-Van Mil, Switzerland 2001

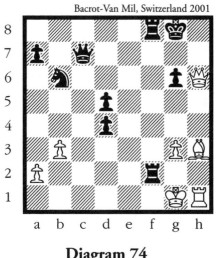

Diagram 74

Your Solution:

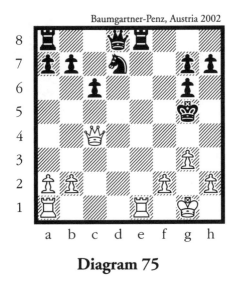

Baumgartner-Penz, Austria 2002

Diagram 75

Your Solution:

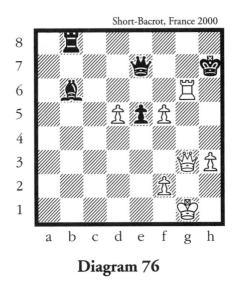

Short-Bacrot, France 2000

Diagram 76

Your Solution:

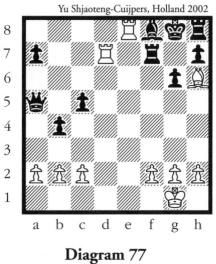

Yu Shjaoteng-Cuijpers, Holland 2002

Diagram 77

Your Solution:

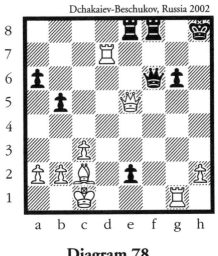

Dchakaiev-Beschukov, Russia 2002

Diagram 78

Your Solution:

Clery-Flament, France 2001

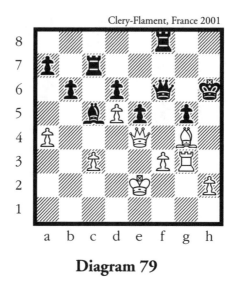

Diagram 79

Your Solution:

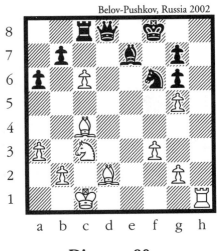

Belov-Pushkov, Russia 2002

Diagram 80

Your Solution:

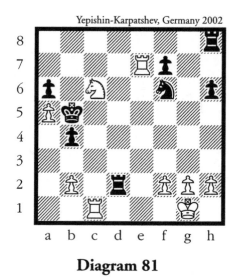

Yepishin-Karpatshev, Germany 2002

Diagram 81

Your Solution:

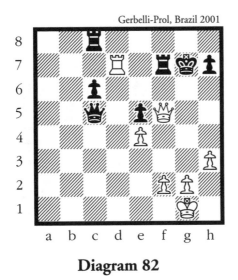

Gerbelli-Prol, Brazil 2001

Diagram 82

Your Solution:

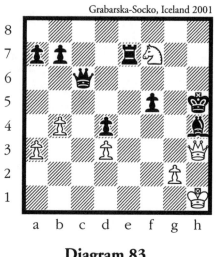

Grabarska-Socko, Iceland 2001

Diagram 83

Your Solution:

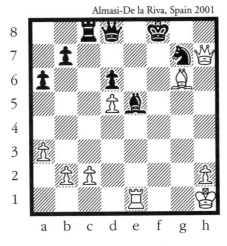

Almasi-De la Riva, Spain 2001

Diagram 84

Your Solution:

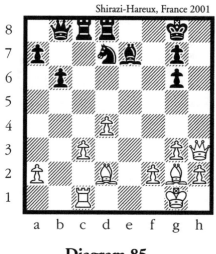

Shirazi-Hareux, France 2001

Diagram 85

Your Solution:

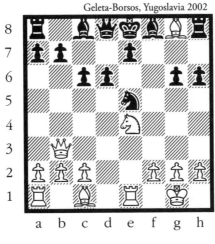

Geleta-Borsos, Yugoslavia 2002

Diagram 86

Your Solution:

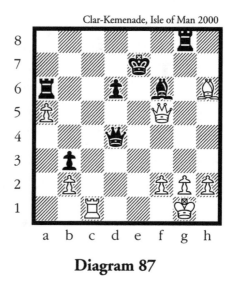

Clar-Kemenade, Isle of Man 2000

Diagram 87

Your Solution:

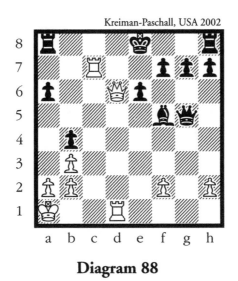

Kreiman-Paschall, USA 2002

Diagram 88

Your Solution:

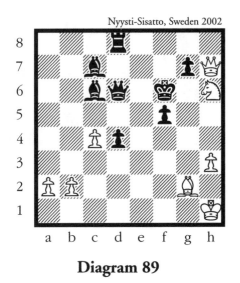

Nyysti-Sisatto, Sweden 2002

Diagram 89

Your Solution:

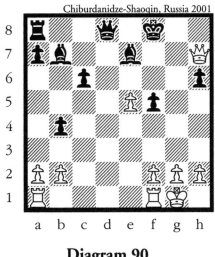

Chiburdanidze-Shaoqin, Russia 2001

Diagram 90

Your Solution:

Pahtz-Radziewicz, Russia 2001

Diagram 91

Your Solution:

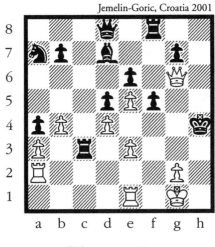

Jemelin-Goric, Croatia 2001

Diagram 92

Your Solution:

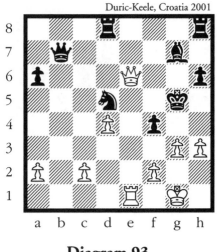

Duric-Keele, Croatia 2001

Diagram 93

Your Solution:

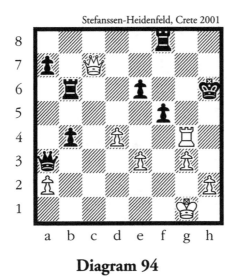

Stefanssen-Heidenfeld, Crete 2001

Diagram 94

Your Solution:

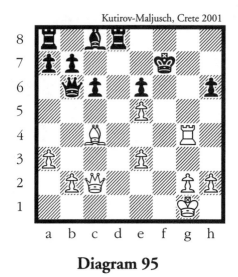

Kutirov-Maljusch, Crete 2001

Diagram 95

Your Solution:

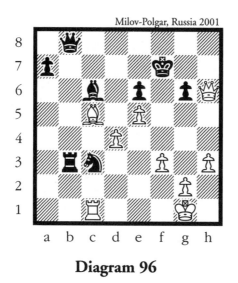

Milov-Polgar, Russia 2001

Diagram 96

Your Solution:

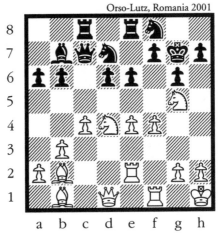

Orso-Lutz, Romania 2001

Diagram 97

Your Solution:

A FEW MORE CHALLENGES

As a last challenge, try these three examples. Each one requires more than two moves for mate.

Schafer-Radice, Bratto 2001

Diagram 98

Your Solution: (three moves for mate)

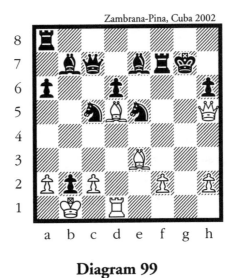

Diagram 99

Your Solution: (four moves for mate)

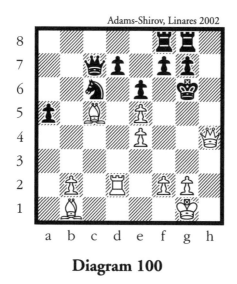

Adams-Shirov, Linares 2002

Diagram 100

Your Solution: (five moves for mate)

SOLUTIONS

1.   1. Queen to f6.
The only way to attack the Black king and prevent its escape.

2.   1. Queen to h7 does the trick.
The rook defends the queen from being captured by the Black king.

3.   1. Bishop to f7.
The bishop is backed up by the rook on f1.

4.   1. Queen to f8.
The king has nowhere to flee and nothing to interpose.

5.   1. Rook to h6.
The king is blocked by his own rook.

6.   1. Queen to f8.
The queen is backed up by the bishop, and once again the king's escape route is blocked by its own pawns.

7.   1. Knight to d5.
An unusual predicament where both knights participate in the king's demise.

8.   1. Bishop takes e6.
This simple capture enables both bishops to rake the board.

9.   1. Knight to e8.
The knight now prevents the king from escaping on c7.

10.   1. Rook to g8 or 1. Pawn on h4 to h5.
Either the rook or pawn administers the fatal dose.

11.   1. Queen takes g7.
Snatching this bishop seals Black's fate.

12.   1. Rook takes f8.
The knight can't recapture – it is pinned to the king by the rook on h4.

13.   1. Pawn on e6 goes to e7.
This lowly pawn is guarded by the rook, which in turn is guarded by the bishop on b2.

14.   1. Queen to g7.
The pawn on f6 not only guards the queen, he also prevents the king from escaping to e7.

15.   1. Queen takes g7.
A crude capture ends all resistance.

16.   1. Queen to f8.
The knight controls h7. It's defended by the pawn on h4.

17.   1. Queen to f8 or 1. Queen takes h7.
Sometimes there is more than one way to skin a cat.

18.   1. Queen to h8.
The king's escape is thwarted by the pawn on f4.

19.   1. Bishop takes e6.
The virtue of this capture is that it stops the king from getting to g8.

20.   1. Knight to f6.
The knights do their dirty work despite the absence of White's queen.

21.   1. Knight to c6.
Once again the knight proves its potency.

22.   1. Knight on d6 to f5.
The other knight is needed on e7 to control both g8 and g6.

23.   1. Queen to f5.
The pawn on e3 keeps the king from fleeing to d4.

24.   1. Rook to h3.
Strike while the iron is hot. The queen can't interpose because it is pinned. Why not move the queen to h5 for check? Because Black would move *his* queen to h6!

25.　　1. Rook to h5.
There's just one way to administer check, but it's fatal!

26.　　1. Bishop to f8.
The king can't take the rook – it's defended by the pawn on f4.

27.　　1. Rook to g8.
A lethal combination of rook and bishop.

28.　　1. Queen to h8.
In many games an open h-file leads to disaster.

29.　　1. Rook to g8.
This rook illustrates the danger of Black's weak back rank.

30.　　1. Bishop to f8.
　　　　　King to g8.
　　　　2. Bishop to h6.

31.　　1. Queen takes g6 – check.
　　　　　Rook takes g6.
　　　　2. Knight to f5.
Sometimes it pays to give a little to get a lot. Giving up the queen clears f5 for the final knight thrust.

32.　　1. Rook takes h6 – check.
　　　　　Pawn on g-file takes h6.
　　　　2. Queen to e5.
The king no longer has any shelter from its pawn.

33.   1. Rook takes f6 – check.
           Pawn on g-file takes f6.
        2. Bishop to h6.
        OR
        1. Rook takes f6 – check.
           Bishop takes f6.
        2. Queen to f7.

The rook can be captured in two ways, each leading to a different mate.

34.   1. Queen takes h7 – check.
           Knight takes h7.
        2. Rook takes h7.

A raw display of brute force along the open h-file. If you don't use it, you lose it!

35.   1. Rook to f5 forces Black's pawn to take f5.
        2. Rook takes f5.

36.   1. Queen takes h7 – check.
           King takes h7.
        2. Rook to h3.

The knight prevents the king from retreating to g8.

37.   1. Rook to h7 – check.
           King takes h7.
        2. Queen to g7.

An old fashioned slam-dunk along the open g-file.

38.   1. Queen to g8 – check.
      Rook takes g8.
    2. Knight to f7.
This is called a "smothered mate," because the king is
hemmed in (smothered) by its own forces.

39.   1. Knight on e4 to g3 – check.
      King to g4.
    2. Bishop to f3.
    OR
    1. Knight on e4 to g3 – check.
      King to f6.
    2. Knight on g5 to e4.
Black can choose his own poison.

40.   1. Bishop to d5.
      Pawn on a2 to a1 (becomes a queen).
    2. Bishop to f3.
It's quite rare for a quiet first move to seal Black's fate.
    OR
    1. Bishop to c4.
      Pawn to a1 (becomes a queen).
    2. Bishop to e2.
Again Black perishes along the d1-h5 diagonal.

41.   1. Pawn on f5 to f6 – check.
      Bishop takes f6.
    2. Pawn on g-file takes f6.
A pawn provides the final thrust of the dagger.

SOLUTIONS

42.   1. Queen to g4 – check.
          King to h6.
     2. Knight to f5.
     OR
     1. Queen to f5 – check.
        King to h6.
     2. Knight to f7.

43.   1. Rook takes g6 – check.
          Pawn on h-file takes g6.
     2. Queen to h8.

The rook sac forces open the h-file while the knight prevents an escape to f7.

44.   1. Knight to e5 – check.
          King to h8 or to f8.
     2. Knight to g6.

Black has no place to hide.

45.   1. Queen takes h6 – check.
          King to g8.
     2 Queen takes g7.

The pawn can't take the queen because it is pinned by the bishop on f6.
     OR
     1. Queen takes h6 – check.
        Queen interposes on h2.
     2. Bishop takes g7.

46.   1. Bishop to f6 – check.
         Knight to g7.
      2. Bishop takes g7.
      OR
      1. Bishop to f6 – check.
         Knight takes f6.
      2. Knight takes g6.

This time the pawn on h7 is pinned and can't take the knight.

47.   1. Knight to f7 – check.
         Rook takes f7.
      2. Rook to g8.

The knight is offered in order to ventilate the g-file.

48.   1. Queen takes h5 – check.
         King takes h5.
      2. Rook to h7.
      OR
      1. Queen takes h5 – check.
         Knight takes h5.
      2. Rook on g1 to g6.
      OR
      1. Queen takes f4 – check.
         Pawn on e5 takes f4.
      2. Rook on g1 to g6.

In any of these ways, offering the queen deflects the king.

49.   1. Rook to f8 – check.
         Bishop to g8.
      2. Rook takes g8.

White goes straight for the jugular.

SOLUTIONS

50.   1. Rook takes f8 – check.

          King takes f8 (forced; the rook is pinned).

       2. Queen to h8.

Notice how all White's forces join in the attack. Even the innocuous bishop on g5 stops the king from reaching e7.

51.   1. Rook takes h6 – check.

          King takes h6.

       2. Queen to h5.

Another win by pin. The queen can't take the rook because it is illegal to leave g7.

52.   1. Rook to g1 – check.

          King to f7.

       2. Queen to g7.

Once again illustrates the danger once a king has been stripped of its pawns on an open file.

53.   1. Queen to g6 – check.

          King to h8.

       2. Bishop takes f6.

       OR

       1. Bishop takes pawn on f6 (a quiet move).

          Rook captures bishop on d5.

       2. Queen goes to g7 or h8.

Black resigned without waiting.

54.   1. Rook to c8 – check.

          King to d7.

       2. Queen to b7.

Straightforward and to the point.

55.   1. Rook to h6 – check.
             Pawn on g-file takes h6.
         2. Queen to g8.
The idea is to remove the last pawn sheltering the king.

56.   1. Queen to f8 – check.
             Rook takes f8.
         2. Pawn on f6 moves to f7.
The clearance sacrifice of the queen makes the bishop on
d4 all-powerful. A slower method is:
         1. Queen to g7 – check.
             Rook takes g7.
         2. Pawn on f6 takes g7 – check.
             King to g8.
         3. Rook to f8.

57.   1. Queen takes h8 – check.
             Knight takes h8.
         2. Rook takes h8.
Notice how the pawn on f6 nixes any escape to e7.

58.   1. Queen to g4 – check.
             King to f6.
         2. Queen to g5.
The pawn on d5 plays a major role in controlling e6.

59.   1. Knight to g8 – check.
             King to g5.
         2. Pawn to f4.
The king can neither advance nor go back.

SOLUTIONS

60.   1. The g-file pawn takes f6 – check.
King to f8.
2. Rook to h8.

OR

1. The e-file pawn takes f6 – check.
King to f8 (the only defense).
2. Rook to h8.

Once again the rook shows its power on an open file.

61.   1. Queen takes g6 – check.
King takes h4.
2. Rook to f4.

White sacrificed most of his pieces to exploit the denuded king.

62.   1. Rook to h4.
Queen takes h4 (what else?)
2. Queen to g7.

The point is to kill the king, not to capture the queen.

63.   1. Rook takes h6 – check.
King takes h6.
2. Queen to g6.

OR

1. Rook takes h6 – check.
Pawn on g-file takes h6.
2. Queen takes g8.

Without this resource White would be stymied.

64.   1. Queen to f6 – check.
        King to h6 or h7.
    2. Rook to h1.
    OR
    1. Queen to e7 – check.
        King to h6 or h8.
    2. Rook to h1.

Another cautionary tale of what can happen on an open h-file.

65.   1. Pawn to g4 – check.
        King to h4.
    2. Rook to h6.

Nothing fancy. Direct and fatal.

66.   1. Queen to c5 – check.
        King to a4.
    2. Pawn to b3 (or Rook to c4).

Danger always lurks after a king strays too far into enemy territory when big guns are still on the board.

67.   1. Queen to g7 – check.
        Queen to f7.
    2. Queen takes f7.

The silent rook on d1 plays a critical role in stopping the king from crossing over to the queenside.

68.   1. Rook to c8 – check.
        Rook to d8.
    2. Rook takes d8 (either one).

Point, set, match.

69.   1. Queen takes e5 – check.
        King to h7.
    2. Queen takes h5.
More succinct than:
        1. Queen takes h5 – check.
        Queen to h7.
        2. Queen takes e5 – check.
        Queen to g7.
        3. Queen takes g7.
That sequence would delay mate by one move.

70.   1. Queen to h6.
        Any move.
    2. Queen to g7.
Once again a quiet first move is decisive. A "quiet" move is one that doesn't contain a capture or a check.

71.   1. Queen to g4 – check.
        King takes f6.
    2. Rook to h6.
    OR
    1. Rook to h5 – check.
        King takes f6.
    2. Queen to g5.
Once again brute forces decides the issue.

72.   1. Knight to d7 – check.
        Knight takes d7.
    2. Queen to g8.
Black's knight was compelled to relinquish defense of g8.

73.   1. Queen to f8 – check.
           Rook to g8.
       2. Bishop to e5.
       OR
       1. Bishop to e5.
           Queen to g6.
       2. Queen to f8.
       OR
       1. Queen to d8 – check.
           Rook interposes to g8.
       2. Bishop to e5.

Needless to say, Black resigned before White had a chance to exercise any of these options.

74.   1. Bishop to e6 – check.
           Rook to f7.
       2. Queen to h8.

Black was forced to block his only escape square on f7 before White could utilize the lethal h-file.

75.   1. Queen to h4 – check.
           King to f5.
       2. Queen to f4.

Alas, the king is forced to go where it doesn't want to go.

76.   1. Rook to h6 – check.
           King takes h6.
       2. Queen to g6.

This clearance sacrifice sets up a one-two punch.

SOLUTIONS

77.   1. Rook takes f8 – check.
          Rook takes f8.
        2. Rook to g7.
The king's path is obstructed by its own men.

78.   1. Queen to h5 – check.
          Pawn on g-file to h5.
        2. Rook to h7.
        OR
        1. Queen to h5 – check.
          King to g8.
        2. Queen to h7.
The distant bishop on c2 enforces its will by guarding the rook on h7.

79.   1. Rook to h3 – check.
          King to g7.
        2. Queen to h7.
Sometimes "always check, it might be mate" works like a charm.

80.   1. Rook to h8 – check.
          Knight to g8.
        2. Rook takes g8.
The same goes for this marauding rook which eats everything in its path.

81.   1. Rook to b7 – check.
          King to a4.
        2. Rook takes b4.
Nothing fancy, just a brutal massacre.

82.   1. Rook takes f7 – check.
                King to h6.
             2. Rook takes h7.
             OR
             1. Rook takes f7 – check.
                King to g8 or h8.
             2. Queen takes h7.

83.   1. Queen takes f5 – check.
                Bishop to g5.
             2. Queen takes g5.

Interposing the bishop merely delays the inevitable.

84.   1. Queen to h8 – check.
                King to e7.
             2. Queen takes g7.

The bishop can't take the queen because it's pinned by the distant rook on e1.

85.   1. Bishop to d5 – check.
                King to f8.
             2. Queen to h8.

This typical mating pattern repeats itself in many games.

86.   1. Knight to f6 – check.
                Pawn on e-file takes f6.
             2. Queen to f7.

An unusual pin. It's taboo for the knight to take the queen in view of the rook lurking on e1.

SOLUTIONS

87.   1. Rook to c7 – check.
             King to d8 or e8.
           2. Queen to d7.
Black has an extra rook, but riches cannot stave off defeat.

88.   1. Queen to d7 – check.
             King to f8.
           2. Queen takes f7.
Simple. Direct. Irrefutable.

89.   1. Queen takes f5 – check.
             King to e7.
           2. Queen to f7.
The king is trapped in the center of the board.

90.   1. Pawn to e6.
             Queen to e8 (how else to stop 2. Queen to f7?)
           2. Queen to h8.
A quiet pawn advance is the only way to force mate.

91.   1. Bishop to h6 – check.
             Rook takes h6.
           2. Queen to g7.
If Black had played King takes f7, White could have mated with Queen to g6. The initial move here is hard to find – yet another example of the power of attack along an open g-file.

92.   1. Pawn to g3 – check.
             King to h3.
           2. Rook to h2.
The king receives no help from its distant couriers.

93.   1. Pawn to h4 – check.
          King to h5.
      2. Queen to f5.
Again a lowly pawn plays a decisive role.

94.   1. Queen to g7 – check.
          King to h5.
      2. Rook to h4 or g5, or Queen to g5 or g6.
All roads lead to Rome.

95.   1. Queen to h7 – check.
          King to e8 or f8.
      2. Rook to g8.
A typical back rank fiasco.

96.   1. Queen to h7 – check.
          King to e8.
      2. Queen to e7.
White's bishop guards the queen at its final destination.

97.   1. Knight to f5 – check.
          King to g8.
      2. Knight to h6.
White's first move is known as a double check because it also unleashes a threat from the bishop on b2.

98.   1. Knight to g7 – check.
          King to h4.
      2. Queen to f2 – check.
          King to g4.
      3. Queen to f4 (or g3).

OR

1. Knight to g7 – check.
   King to h4.
2. Queen takes h6 – check.
   King to g4.
3. Rook to f4.

99. 1. Queen takes h6 – check.
   King to g8.
2. Rook to g1 – check.
   Knight to g4.
3. Rook takes g4 – check.
   Bishop to g5.
4. Rook takes g5.

Black can delay his doom only by interposing pieces in vain. Black saw it coming and resigned first.

100. 1. Queen to g4 – check.
   King to h6 (Black doesn't play into White's plot with King to h7, so White could play Queen to h5).
2. Bishop to e3 – check.
   Pawn to g5.
3. Queen to h4 – check.
   King to g6.
4. Queen takes g5 – check.
   King to h7.
5. Queen to h6.

Stubborn defense often is overcome by a stubborn attack.

NOTES

MORE CARDOZA TITLES

- BEGINNING AND GENERAL CHESS BOOKS -

BEGINNING CHESS PLAY by Bill Robertie - Step-by-step approach uses 113 diagrams to teach the basics of chess: opening, middle and endgame strategies, principles of development, pawn structure, checkmates, openings and defenses, how to write and read chess notation, join a chess club, play in tournaments, use a chess clock, and get rated. Two annotated games illlustrate strategic thinking for easy learning. 144 pages, $9.95.

COMPLETE BOOK OF BEGINNING CHESS by Raymond Keene - Complete step-by-step course shows how to play and deepen one's understanding of chess. Fascinating chapters on chess heroes and the lessons one can learn from them, basic chess openings, strategy, tactics, the best games of chess ever played, and the history of chess. Learn how to use chess notation and all the basic concepts of game play – castling, pawn promotion, checking an opponent, the five ways of drawing or stalemating games, en passant, checkmate, and much more. 320 pgs, $19.95.

OFFICIAL RULES OF CHESS Professional, Scholastic, and Internet Chess Rules Eric Schiller and Richard Peterson - This is the official new guide to the professional, scholastic, amateur, and internet rules of chess. Learn everything you need to know about tournaments, rating systems, etiquette for in-person and online play, chess notation, and the rules that apply to every tournament form of chess, from scholastic competitions to World Championship play. Endorsed by the CEA, the official body for U.S. scholastic chess. 96 pgs, $9.95.

WHIZ KIDS TEACH CHESS Eric Schiller & the Whiz Kids - Today's greatest young stars, some perhaps to be future world champions, present a fascinating look at the world of chess. Each tells of their successes, failures, world travels, and love of chess, show off their best moves, and admit to their most embarrassing blunders. This is more than just a fascinating look at prodigies like Vinay Bhat and Irina Krush, it's also a primer featuring diagrams, explanations, and winning ideas for young players. 144 oversized pages, $14.95.

- OPENING STRATEGY -

COMPLETE DEFENSE TO KING PAWN OPENINGS by Eric Schiller - Learn a complete defensive system against 1.e4. This powerful repertoire not only limits White's ability to obtain any significant opening advantage but allows Black to adopt the flexible Caro-Kann formation, the favorite weapon of many of the greatest chess players. All White's options are explained in detail, and a plan is given for Black to combat them all. Analysis is up-to-date and backed by examples drawn from games of top stars. Detailed index lets you follow the opening from the point of a specific player, or through its history. 240 pages, $18.95.

COMPLETE DEFENSE TO QUEEN PAWN OPENINGS by Eric Schiller - This aggressive counterattacking repertoire covers Black opening systems against virtually every chess opening except for 1.e4 (including most flank games), based on the exciting and powerful Tarrasch Defense, an opening that helped bring Championship titles to Kasparov and Spassky. Black learns to effectively use the Classical Tarrasch, Symmetrical Tarrasch, Asymmetrical Tarrasch, Marshall and Tarrasch Gambits, and Tarrasch without Nc3, to achieve an early equality or even an outright advantage in the first few moves. 288 pages, $16.95.

GAMBIT OPENING REPERTOIRE FOR BLACK by Eric Schiller - For players that like exciting no-holds-barred chess, this versatile gambit repertoire shows Black how to take charge with aggressive attacking defenses against any orthodox White opening move; 1.e4, 1.d4 and 1.c4. Learn the Scandinavian Gambit against 1.e4, the Schara Gambit and Queen's Gambit Declined variations against 1.d4, and some flank and unorthodox gambits also. Black learns the secrets of seizing the initiative from White's hands, usually by investing a pawn or two, to begin powerful attacks that can send White to early defeat. 176 pgs, $14.95.

GAMBIT OPENING REPERTOIRE FOR WHITE by Eric Schiller - Chessplayers who enjoy attacking from the very first move are rewarded here with a powerful repertoire of brilliant gambits. Starting off with 1.e4 or 1.d4 and then using such sharp weapons such as the Göring Gambit (Accepted and Declined), Halasz Gambit, Alapin Gambit, Ulysses Gambit, Short Attack and many more to put great pressure on opponents. You'll learn a complete attacking repertoire to use against popular defenses such as the Sicilian, French, Scandinavian, Caro-Kann, Pirc, Alekhine, and other Open Game positions. 192 pgs, $14.95.

HYPERMODERN OPENING REPERTOIRE FOR WHITE by Eric Schiller - This complete opening repertoire for White shows how to stun opponents by "allowing" Black to occupy the center with its pawns, while building a crushing phalanx from the flanks, ready to smash the center apart with Black's slightest mistake. White's approach is easy to learn because White almost always develops pieces in the same manner, but can be used against all defenses no matter what Black plays! Diagrams and explanations illustrate every concept. The Réti and English openings, which form the basis of the Hypermodern, lead to lively games with brilliant sacrifices and subtle maneuvering. 304 pgs, $16.95..

WINNING CHESS OPENINGS by Bill Robertie - Shows concepts and best opening moves of more than 25 openings from Black's and White's perspectives: King's Gambit, Center Game, Scotch Game, Giucco Piano, Vienna Game, Bishop's Opening, Ruy Lopez, French, Caro-Kann, Sicilian, Alekhine, Pirc, Modern, Queen's Gambit, Nimzo-Indian, Queen's Indian, Dutch, King's Indian, Benoni, English, Bird's, Reti's, and King's Indian Attack. Examples from 25 grandmasters and champions. 144 pages, $9.95

- OPENING REFERENCE -

GAMBIT CHESS OPENINGS (GCO) by Eric Schiller - Gambits, where one side sacrifices material for an advance in development, are the most exciting and popular openings in chess! GCO presents every important gambit opening and variation ever played and currently in vogue – more than 2,000 opening strategies in all! Each gambit is covered in detail with a diagram showing the standard position representative of the gambit, the move orders taken to reach there, and an explanation in plain language of the thinking behind the moves. More than 100 complete games are included so that you can see how the ideas behind the gambit are influential all the way through a game. 784 pgs, $24.95.

STANDARD CHESS OPENINGS (SCO) by Eric Schiller - This comprehensive guide covers every important chess opening and variation ever played and currently in vogue. In all, more than 3,000 opening strategies are presented!

MORE CARDOZA TITLES

Differing from previous opening books which rely almost exclusively on bare notation, SCO features substantial discussion and analysis on each opening so that you learn and understand the concepts behind them. Includes more than 250 completely annotated games (including a game representative of each major opening) and more than 1,000 diagrams! This is the standard reference book necessary for competitive play. A must have for chess players!!! 768 pgs, $24.95

UNORTHODOX CHESS OPENINGS by Eric Schiller - The exciting guide to all the major unorthodox openings used by chess players, contains more than 1,500 weird, contentious, controversial, unconventional, arrogant, and outright strange opening strategies. From their tricky tactical surprises to their bizarre names, these openings fly in the face of tradition. You'll meet such openings as the Orangutang, Raptor Variation, Halloween Gambit, Double Duck, Frankenstein-Dracula Variation, and even the Drunken King! These openings are a great weapon to spring on unsuspecting and often unprepared opponents. More than 750 diagrams show essential positions. 528 pages, $24.95

QUALITY BACKGAMMON SETS

Get ready to play backgammon and improve your game. These deluxe backgammon sets come complete with Uria checkers, dice, and dice cups. Dimensions given with the case closed.

PLAYER SET

Quality velour-covered field plus smart touches of leatherette points are housed in a handsome velour exterior case with solid brass latches .

Regular size
18" x 12" size - $69.95

The Player Set

VISCOUNT

For real looks and playing pleasure, the Viscount comes with genuine leather exterior, suede field, and solid brass latches.

Tournament size
18 1/2" x 12 1/2" - $99.95

The Viscount

PLAY BACKGAMMON WITH THESE BEAUTIFUL SETS!

Let's Play! Enclosed is a check or money order made out to Cardoza Publishing for the desired items above. Shipping charges are listed below.

Cardoza Publishing, P.O. Box 1500, Cooper Station, New York, NY 10276

Call Toll-Free in U.S. & Canada: 1-800-577-WINS

Please include $10.00 postage/handling for U.S. orders; CANADA/MEXICO double; other countries 4X. Orders outside U.S., money order payable in U.S. dollars on U. S. bank only.

Indicate desired item(s): _____   _____

NAME _____

ADDRESS _____

CITY _____ STATE _____ ZIP _____

Order Today! 30 Day Money Back Guarantee!   Evans2003